C000157446

BE A BETTER
LITERACY COORDINATOR

Roger Hurn

Other titles in this series

BE A BETTER
LITERACY COORDINATOR

by Roger Hurn

TEACH
BOOKS

A division of MA Education Ltd

Teach Books Division, MA Education Ltd, St Jude's Church, Dulwich Road, London SE24 0PB

British Library Cataloguing-in-Publication Data
A catalogue record is available for this book

© MA Education Limited 2006
ISBN 1 85642 321 2

Printed in the UK by Athenaeum Press Ltd, Dukesway, Team Valley, Gateshead, NE11 0PZ

CONTENTS

INTRODUCTION

You love books. You get excited by a good story. You enjoy the process of writing and you want others to share your enthusiasm for literacy. You're someone who sees children's minds as fires to be lit and not as buckets to be filled. That's why you're a literacy coordinator. But, because you know that a good teacher is someone who never ceases to learn, you want to find ways to improve how you go about bringing literacy alive. Well, this book is designed to help you do just that.

So what are the key principles that you should keep in mind on your quest to become a better literacy coordinator? Perhaps the most important one is that you are not alone. It is not your job to carry the torch for literacy in the school single-handedly. Many, if not all, of your colleagues will already be engaged in good literacy practice. Be ready to listen to and act on their ideas as well as to offer insights of your own. You will have a real impact on standards of teaching and learning if your fellow teachers see you as someone who, although a specialist in the subject, still recognises and acknowledges their experience and expertise. People are always more receptive to initiatives if they feel the person introducing the new ideas, strategies and approaches values them as professionals.

Obviously, your ideas about developing literacy will have a greater chance of taking root if your colleagues do respect your expertise and knowledge. In order for this to happen, you have to have a clear picture of the state of literacy teaching and learning in your school so that you can identify strengths and weaknesses and offer appropriate support and guidance where it's needed. To do this effectively you must have a well-defined system of monitoring and assessment, as well as practical strategies and solutions that your colleagues can adapt to enhance the quality of their literacy lessons.

You will also need to keep yourself informed about the latest advances in the teaching of literacy so that you can see how they can best serve the aims of your school's literacy development. However, always take the time to consider the implications of these ideas and how they will impact on the school's resources and, more importantly, the teachers' time, before you disseminate them to your staff. You may find the ideas exciting and innovative, but your colleagues already have a heavy workload and they may resent yet another new initiative being thrust on them. Therefore, choose your moment to introduce novel ideas with care. You want to inspire your colleagues, not overwhelm them.

However, you can avoid the pitfalls of curriculum overload if you have a plan. Well, several plans actually – short-, medium- and long-term – as these will help you track what's going on in literacy in your school from the nursery right up to year 6. Make sure all your colleagues have an input into these plans so that everyone knows how, when and what they are expected to achieve in their literacy teaching.

At this point you may be thinking that all this is easy to say but a lot harder to do. That's a fair point. So let's get down to practicalities, and what could be more practical than working with pupils, which just happens to be the title of Chapter One.

CHAPTER ONE

WORKING WITH PUPILS

In your school, no matter what its size or setting, the children will have a wide range of abilities, attitudes and interests when it comes to literacy. Some will arrive with a built-in love of books while others may not even be able to write their own names. However, it is your job as literacy coordinator to help each and every one of these children develop their knowledge and skills, so that they achieve to the best of their ability while they are in your care. Obviously, you are someone who wants to be a better literacy coordinator. Therefore your aim will be to foster in them a lifelong love of literature. At the very least you will want to ensure that, by the time they leave your school, they have gained a competence and confidence in reading, writing and their ability to express themselves which will always stand them in good stead. The question is: how do you go about achieving this laudable aim?

MOTIVATION

Well let's start, as all good educationalists do, with the child. All children need to be inspired and motivated if they are to learn. As Sir John Lubbock (1834-1913) once said, 'If we succeed in giving the love of learning, the learning itself is sure to follow.' Sir John may have been an eminent Victorian naturalist, but I'm sure all of us involved in teaching today will agree that this statement is as true now as it was then. Of course, the best way to instil that love of learning is to create a learning environment for literacy that is rich and stimulating. Here are five key ways in which this can be done:

- Create a print-rich environment in your school by having attractive displays and posters promoting all aspects of literacy, writers and books.
- Ensure that your school library is welcoming and well-stocked, as it is the perfect place for exciting a child's imagination and leading them on to an appreciation and love of books.
- Set up a system of 'book buddies'.
- Arrange a regular programme of author visits.
- Use events such as World Book Day to turn your whole school into a wonderland of fun activities which have books as their focus.

A print-rich environment

Make sure the displays are interactive and have questions that invite and encourage children to stop, look, think and read. All children have a natural curiosity and will respond to questions such as:

> 'What meat-eater stood over 6 metres tall, weighed 7 tons and had teeth 18 centimetres long? Well, it's hiding inside one of these books. Can you track it down?'

Alternatively, you may want to set up a quiz corner, well stocked with reference books and magazines, where children are challenged to find answers to a whole range of questions such as:

> What is the biggest planet in the solar system?
> Which bird lays the largest eggs?
> What is the world's longest river?

You may want, if space allows, to provide bean-bag chairs by the displays so that children can sit comfortably while they engage in their quest for knowledge.

This method of stimulating critical thinking, discussion and written work on the part of all the children can be developed by taking an odd or unusual object into assembly. This could be, for example, a small piece of machinery encased inside a large plastic egg. Tell the children that you found this mysterious object in your garden, attic or shed. Say that the other teachers are baffled by it. Explain that you will place the object on display in a prominent position in the school and you want the children, over the next week or so, to write their suggestions as to what it is on the sheets of paper provided. You can put the most interesting and imaginative responses up for everyone to read and the children can vote for the explanation they think most likely. Children respond enthusiastically to this activity and their responses are nearly always imaginative and entertaining. Don't worry if you haven't got an 'alien' style egg to hand, any weird and wonderful object will work just as well.

The school library

You will never inspire the children or motivate them to immerse themselves in the world of books if your school library is a dull, dingy place stocked with books that are well past their sell-by date. We'll take a closer and more detailed look at how to make the most of your school library in a later chapter, but here are a few quick things to look for to check whether it is a child-friendly place.

- Is it bright and colourful with plenty of interesting posters promoting authors and books?
- Are there large welcome signs that invite the children to come in and use the place?
- Are there straightforward, easy-to-read instructions, labels and directions showing how and where to find the books the children want?
- Are there comfortable floor cushions, computers, plants, tables and chairs so that children can use the library for a variety of purposes?
- Does it contain regularly changing displays that focus on different aspects of literacy?
- Does the library publicise local literacy events that may interest the children?

If you can say yes to all of the above questions, the chances are your library is a thriving place which the children use because they recognise its value and enjoy spending time in it.

Book buddies

Many older children take great delight in helping younger children to read. It gives them a sense that they are making a positive and worthwhile contribution. It also reinforces their self-confidence by confirming that they have mastered the art of reading themselves. Younger children enjoy the time they spend reading with their book buddies. They often find it a less stressful way of practising new skills than attempting to read with an adult. Of course, it is advisable for you to give the older children some simple tips and advice on how to share books and encourage reading before you team them up with their young 'buddies'. However, if you do take the time to do this, you'll find that you've set in motion a system that promotes a feeling of togetherness and shared purpose, and one that helps foster a very positive attitude towards reading throughout the school.

Author visits

There is nothing more guaranteed to make children realise that books and stories are enormous fun than to have professional writers and storytellers make regular visits to your school. As it says in the Writing Together Conference Report (Qualifications and Curriculum Authority (QCA) *et al*, 2001)

> '... *we believe that the opportunity to work with a professional writer in school can be a real inspiration for many children. It can give them unique insights into where writers get their ideas, how they develop and refine them, how they take their readers into account and how they work with illustrators and publishers.*'

Storytellers take a slightly different, but none the less valuable, tack. By using their oracy skills they can take children out of the mundane world of everyday existence and off on a journey of the imagination. They also provide a role model for the children when it comes to enhancing speaking and listening skills. Indeed there's no more certain way to inspire the children in your school to want to write or tell stories themselves than by letting them spend time in the company of people who earn their living in this way.

5

World Book Day

To paraphrase a well-known slogan, 'Books are for life and not just for World Book Day'. However, events such as World Book Day can be extremely useful in your efforts to motivate the children to speak and listen and read and write. If you don't know what it is, then let me explain. It's the biggest celebration of all things to do with books and reading in the UK. It's organised jointly by the Publishers Association and the Booksellers Association who will send you a pack full of information, tips and ideas for making the most of the day and turning even the most reluctant readers onto books.

World Book Day gives you, the staff and the children the perfect opportunity to celebrate all things to do with books. It should provide a focus for a whole range of exciting activities such as bringing favourite storybook characters to life by dressing up as them for the day, inviting poets, authors and storytellers into the school, having teachers share their favourite books with the children and so on. In short, World Book Day should be the outward manifestation of the feel-good factor towards everything to do with literacy which you, as the literacy coordinator, have created in your school.

THE EARLY YEARS

We've looked at ways in which you can motivate and inspire children throughout the school, but now we must examine the area where you will be laying the foundations for building a healthy approach to literacy – the early years.

Over the last few years, pressure has been brought to bear on early years practitioners to teach very young children more formally in order to 'improve' their literacy skills. However, any literacy coordinator worth their salt will give short shrift to any attempts to introduce activities that are inappropriate to the children's intellectual or emotional development. We know that young children learn best through structured play, and few of us would argue with the idea that they should be introduced to the structure of language through games, songs, rhymes and focused talk. But sometimes an early years classroom can be a place where there is plenty of activity going on but very little learning is taking place. As someone who is committed to improving your practice, you will want to know how to turn a classroom that bears more than a passing resemblance to the Tower of Babel into a productive place for nurturing, developing and extending language skills. So you need to begin by taking a closer look at how the children are playing together and how the adults in the class are interacting with them.

Spontaneous play

If you set up a classroom and fill it with interesting objects and areas for the children to use and explore, they will certainly initiate their own play activities. But these can often degenerate into petty squabbles, and that's no fun for anyone. You can avoid this and still allow them to engage in spontaneous, child-generated games by first teaching them the concepts of taking turns and listening to others, as outlined in the Curriculum guidance for the foundation stage (QCA, 2000). By doing so, you'll ensure that they spend far more time actually engaging with each other in a way that is productive in terms of language development than they will in fussing and arguing.

Talking with children

Children need good role models on which to base their own attempts at developing language. Therefore all adults in an early years classroom need to provide them with exactly that. The following check list gives pointers on how an adult should talk with children:

- Don't shout at the children.
- Use eye contact, physical positioning, body language (such as putting a finger to your lips), facial expression and the children's names to gain and hold their attention.
- When the children are settled and focused on you, remember to speak more slowly than you would if you were speaking to an adult.
- When you talk to the children, use simple sentence construction and vocabulary.
- Establish ground rules for talking, such as only one person speaking at a time.
- Don't dominate the conversation or give out too much information all at once. This limits the children's

opportunities to respond and they will either become bored or disruptive.

- Ask lots of open questions.
- Don't rush the children into giving you an answer. Allow them some thinking time.
- Always respond positively to the answers the children give, even if they have missed the point. They need to be encouraged not crushed.

Creating the optimum conditions for language development

It is a matter of common sense, although research has confirmed it, that opportunities for developing communication and language skills are enhanced when initiated with small groups of children. Naturally, this has implications for how early years classes are organised. You probably already encourage the staff to engage the children in activities such as story time, circle time, show and tell, phonic games, singing games, rhyming games and whole class plenary sessions. These will all reinforce the language learning that has taken place during those activities. However, you may want to consider having, wherever possible, smaller circle times, smaller group outings and smaller groups for show and tell if the children in your school's early years classes are going to extend and develop their language skills in a purposeful way.

HOW CAN YOU INVOLVE CHILDREN IN DEVELOPING THEIR LITERACY SKILLS?

So far we've looked at how you can create a positive ethos in your school towards literacy and how you make sure the children in the early years get off to a good start as far as their language skills are concerned. Now we must turn our attention to how you can turn children from being overly negative about their literacy achievements by engaging them in the activity of self-assessment.

Children, while often quite perceptive about their own capabilities, can often do themselves down by focusing on the more superficial aspects of their work, such as the state of their handwriting or their inability to spell with any degree of accuracy. You can address this problem by showing them how to map and monitor their progress in literacy. Once they become involved in this process the children tend to:

- take more interest in their work
- set themselves realistic and achievable targets
- cooperate with their teachers to attain these targets
- discuss their work with a greater sense of purpose
- ask questions to clarify their understanding
- develop positive strategies for coping with difficulties.

It is never too early to introduce children to the idea of self-assessment. After all, what you are doing is helping children to think critically about their own work and providing them with a very useful tool that will, in time, enable them to become independent learners. It has been said that a good teacher is someone who makes him-/herself progressively unnecessary. By teaching the children the skills of self-assessment you will be going some way to realising this goal. However, these skills take time to master and the children will only do so with your guidance. Begin by being very clear about what your expectations are. Then encourage the children to set small, easily attainable goals that are in keeping with those expectations. Always be quick to congratulate the children when they succeed in reaching them. This positive reinforcement works wonders for their morale and gives them the confidence to try and improve on what they have already achieved. For example, if the children are writing a story you can give them a simple check list (*Box 1.1*) which focuses on the quality of what they've written – rather than their secretarial skills – to use as part of the self-assessment process.

Box 1.1 Story writing check list

Before you share your story with me, see how many of the following questions you can answer yes to:

- Does it have an attention-grabbing beginning?
- Is the setting well described?
- Does your story have lively characters?
- Does it have a good plot?
- Have you kept the action moving?
- Have you used adjectives and adverbs to make your writing exciting?
- Does it all work out at the end?

If you can't tick all the questions have another look at what you've written and see how you can improve it.

CHILDREN WITH ENGLISH AS AN ADDITIONAL LANGUAGE

No discussion of how you work with your pupils would be complete without addressing the issues raised by children for whom English is an additional language (EAL). Perhaps the first thing to stress is that even though some EAL children may have difficulty in expressing themselves in English, this does not mean that they have cognitive problems or lack academic ability. However, if such a child arrives in your school, he or she will see children and teachers happily communicating with each other in a language that s/he cannot yet understand. This may lead children to withdraw into themselves and can undermine their self-confidence. This situation will be exacerbated if s/he is the only speaker of the home language in the school. Thankfully, there are some strategies you can adopt to ameliorate the situation.

Set up a 'buddy' system

Arrange for a popular and confident child who is fluent in English to 'adopt' the new arrival until he or she is able to make friends independently.

Remember how we acquire language

Don't fall into the trap of thinking that children with EAL will learn English more quickly if they are isolated. One-to-one sessions should be short and held on a regular basis. They are not a long-term solution. The only real way to learn a language is to become immersed in it, and the child can only get this by being in the classroom where English is used in context. However, some class teachers might find this a daunting prospect so here are some strategies you can offer them:

- Don't just tell EAL children to do something – demonstrate how it's done.
- Always use visual prompts if possible. Make sure all labels and displays reflect the languages spoken by the children.

- Make speaking and listening the focus of group activity. The process of thinking out loud and talking through ideas is essential to language acquisition.

- Pair the EAL child up with a child who is fluent in English. They will be a good language role model.

- Have a stock of books that reflect the home cultures and countries of EAL children.

- Create an atmosphere of encouragement. Let the children know it's alright to make mistakes.

- Encourage the teachers to let the EAL children teach them how to speak some key words from their home language. It boosts the children's self-esteem and reminds the teacher of what it's like to learn a new language.

- Take extra time and care to explain a new concept to EAL children. The rest of the class will benefit from the reinforcement.

- Give regular feedback about their work to EAL children so they know they're making progress.

- Provide a portfolio of examples of work done by EAL children throughout the school so class teachers have a yardstick to measure the progress made by individual children.

Hopefully, this chapter will have given you plenty of food for thought on how you can motivate and inspire the children in your school to become confident and competent in literacy. But before we move on to Chapter Two - Keeping on top of your subject - why not have a look at the handy hints box to refresh your memory as to what you've read?

Handy Hints

- If we succeed in giving the love of learning, the learning itself is sure to follow.

- Create a rich and stimulating learning environment in all parts of your school.

- Set up a system of 'book buddies'.

- Arrange a regular programme of author visits and use events such as World Book Day to promote love of books.

- Teach young children through games, songs and rhymes and use small groups whenever possible.

- Help children to develop self-assessment so that they may become independent learners.

- EAL (English as an additional language) children will learn English in a real-life context rather than in isolation.

CHAPTER TWO

KEEPING ON TOP OF YOUR SUBJECT

The one thing most teachers complain about is the lack of time they seem to have to do their job in the way they would like. In fact, it's almost impossible to open a newspaper these days without seeing an announcement of another shake-up in the way schools are run or the way children are to be taught. If a week is a long time in politics in general, then it seems it's an age for the DfES (Department for Education and Skills) in particular – and this has led to what some have called 'initiativitis'.

However, teachers are a resourceful lot and have continued to find ways of making sense of the demands made on them. Needless to say though, as literacy is such an essential part of the curriculum, literacy coordinators have had more than their fair share of initiatives to cope with. For example, literacy programmes such as Additional Literacy Support, Early Literacy Support, Progression in Phonics, Grammar for Writing, Developing Early Writing, Further Literacy Support, Booster Groups and Speaking and Listening have all been introduced since the implementation of the National Literacy Strategy. And, as if this wasn't enough, there is always the prospect of an Ofsted inspection to contend with.

On top of all this, as literacy coordinator, you'll need to keep up-to-date with the latest and best quality resources for promoting literacy but, to return to the point made at the start of this chapter, how on earth do you find the time to do that and deal with everything else that's been mentioned? Well, let's see if we can find an effective way for you to stay on top of things. We'll start by examining how best you can manage and monitor the programmes already referred to.

COPING WITH INITIATIVES

The key thing to remember is that teachers are more receptive to new initiatives if:

- It is made explicit exactly what is expected of them.
- They can implement the initiative in a way that builds on what they are already achieving with the children.

This isn't rocket science, but sometimes it's easy to forget that not every member of staff shares your passion for literacy. Teachers need to be approached with sensitivity and tact if they are going to get behind a new initiative and make it work in their classroom. So let's look at each of the initiatives in turn and see how they can be managed appropriately.

Additional Literacy Support

This was aimed initially at those children in years 3 and 4 who were not making the progress expected of them in phonics, reading and writing at this stage in their school career. However, it is now deemed appropriate for children in year 3 only. It's delivered to small groups of children working with a teaching assistant, under the direction of the class teacher, for a series of short, tightly-focused sessions designed to give the children the support they need. However, it must be stressed that the children you choose to benefit from this should not be those for whom literacy is still an undiscovered world, but rather those who are now ready to cope with being taught phonics. In other words, it is for children operating at Level 2c and 3a, i.e. children who have already fallen behind in literacy, but who aren't receiving any additional support in this area. You, as literacy coordinator, need to ensure that all teachers are aware of this if the Additional Literacy Support process is to be successful. Once you've done so, you can easily monitor and assess how well the targeted children are doing by mapping their progress at the end of each unit.

Progression in Phonics

This programme is designed to give a seven-step progression for teaching children the phonic knowledge they'll need to become independent readers and provides the starting point for spelling. With its multi-sensory approach which builds on children's natural curiosity about language and readiness to experiment, explore and play with sounds, Progression in Phonics is ideally suited to the foundation stage. However, it may not fit quite so well into the more formal structure of the literacy hour practised in year I. Therefore, in order to provide continuity of experience, you should try to ensure that your reception and year 1 teachers adopt, as far as possible, similar routines and activities when developing literacy.

In the summer term, it's a good idea to allow the younger children to participate in 'induction' literacy hour style lessons with children from year 1, using activities from Progression in Phonics, as this will help prepare them for the transition to a standard literacy hour.

Grammar for Writing

Not every teacher, or literacy coordinator for that matter, feels totally on top of the nuances and finer points of English grammar. After all, how many of us can explain what a gerund is without resorting to the glossary at the back of the National Literacy Strategy Framework for Teaching document? And even if we did, it wouldn't do us any good as it isn't there. (In case you're interested, it's a word that ends in '-ing' which is made from a verb, and which is used like a noun.) The DfES has recognised this situation and introduced Grammar for Writing to help teachers in key stage 2 feel more secure in what they are teaching. However, not every teacher welcomed it with open arms and many still feel defensive and reluctant to admit to having a lack of confidence in their own grammatical knowledge and skills. So the challenge facing you is how to identify your colleagues who feel this way and help them draw on the advice given in the Grammar for Writing book and video.

The first thing to do is find out if the teachers in key stage 2 are actually using the book to teach grammar. You can do this either through classroom observation (make sure you tell the teachers that you will be focusing on how grammar is taught so that they are prepared) or by checking their literacy planning documents and looking to see if there is evidence that grammar is being taught, either directly during sentence level work or indirectly when children are working independently on literacy activities. If you find that, for whatever reasons, e.g. a newly qualified teacher is taking a year 6 class, it just isn't happening, then you need to act, because knowledge of how language works is essential if children are to master the kind of higher-order literacy skills demanded of them in years 5 and 6.

An effective way of tackling this is to hold a staff meeting where you explore how user-friendly the book is and how easily the suggestions in it can be adapted for use in the classroom. You could also volunteer to work alongside any colleague who feels uncertain about teaching grammar to help them plan and deliver appropriate lessons.

Developing Early Writing

This initiative is aimed at year 2 but is applicable across key stage 1. Again, it is intended to help teachers who are not confident in teaching grammar. In order for you to ensure that children are being taught to help them understand how English is structured, you should adopt the same approach as for checking the implementation of Grammar for Writing:

- monitoring planning
- classroom observation
- staff meetings
- collaborative working.

Early Literacy Support

This initiative involves focusing on a small group of year 1 children which has been identified as needing a more intensive programme of support than the majority of the class. This group needs to master the skills being developed in the literacy hour. As in the Additional Literacy Support programme, these children are assigned a teaching assistant who works with them every day.

However, it is important that you, as literacy coordinator, make sure that the selection criteria for inclusion in this group are strictly adhered to, otherwise the programme will not have the desired effect. It is not a way for harassed class teachers to give themselves, and the rest of the class, a break from the children with emotional and behavioural difficulties. The programme has a specific purpose, which is to locate and support those children who are most at risk of underachieving in terms of their literacy skills and not through their disruptive behaviour.

An excellent way for you to monitor this situation is by attending one of the regular four weekly assessments to check the progress being made by the children in the group. This will give you the opportunity to observe how well the teaching assistant is managing the learning materials and whether or not the children are responding appropriately.

Further Literacy Support

In keeping with its avowed aim of promoting joined-up thinking, the DfES has designed this intervention to build on the work started in the Early and Additional Literacy Support programmes. Indeed, it uses exactly the same model of implementation as Early Literacy Support. While this is laudable, it does have some implications of which you need to be aware. For example, you cannot assume that the children who have previously received literacy support will automatically qualify to receive help again. The class teacher and the teaching assistant must operate the screening process at the end of the autumn term in year 5 and identify those children who will most benefit from the intervention offered.

Sometimes teachers are put under pressure by parents who, worried that their child isn't making the progress they feel s/he should, demand that their child be given extra help by being placed in the Further Literacy Support group. This can be a tricky situation for a class teacher to deal with and so it's likely that the teacher will call on you, in your role as the literacy coordinator, to help them out. This sounds a daunting task, but there's no need to succumb if you have instituted the good management practice of ensuring that all teachers keep their literacy assessment records up-to-date. These records provide you with the data you need to show any interested parties, be they parents, other colleagues or inspectors, that all decisions are firmly based on documentary evidence, not whims.

Speaking and Listening

A major area in which the National Literacy Strategy failed to provide anything like the guidance teachers required was speaking and ilstening. The QCA attempted to address this by issuing, in October 2003, a pack of materials to schools (DfES, 2003). This includes a handbook, an outline of teaching objectives, a video, leaflets and a poster highlighting the importance of speaking and listening. The materials concentrate on four areas of classroom activity: group discussion and interaction, speaking, listening and drama. They include detailed suggestions on how to teach speaking and listening, as well as ideas on how to develop children's oral skills in a cross curricular way.

Obviously, these suggestions and ideas have to be incorporated into the literacy planning which your teachers do. You will undoubtedly have held INSET sessions using the material from the pack, but as the old Chinese proverb has it, 'I hear and I forget, I see and I remember, I do and I understand.' So a good way of disseminating good practice in teaching speaking and listening across the school is to use some of your post holder time to release a teacher who, for example, finds drama difficult to teach effectively. The teacher can then work alongside a colleague who is using the techniques of drama to inspire the children to become more skilled at speaking and listening.

MANAGEMENT IMPLICATIONS

All of the above initiatives should assist you in your drive to raise standards of achievement in literacy but, if you are to stay on top of them, you need to bear in mind three key management issues:

- keeping the channels of communications open
- making sure your teaching assistants are well trained and motivated
- gaining parental support.

Communications

Perhaps it's stating the obvious to say that any initiative will only survive and prosper if everyone involved in its implementation understands:

- why it's important
- what its aims and objectives are
- how it fits into the school's development plan
- what is expected of them in terms of planning and delivery
- exactly what they need to do in order to achieve a successful outcome.

In short, your colleagues need to feel a sense of ownership of the initiative. And it's not just the classroom teachers either.

Don't forget the children, the parents, the teaching assistants, the SENCO (special educational needs coordinator) and anyone else who has a part to play in this enterprise.

Teaching assistants

The success of the Early Literacy Support, Additional Literacy Support and Further Literacy Support programmes is very much dependent on the quality of input given by your teaching assistants. Therefore it's imperative that they are thoroughly familiar with the materials they'll be using and how to use them. They will also need to be able to work closely with the class teachers as well as on their own. But above all, they'll need to be motivated enough to persevere with the task even when the going gets tough. So, how can you ensure that they are?

One simple way is to give them adequate preparation time. Nobody likes to feel they are being thrown in at the deep end or that they are expected to conjure up resources while coping with an eager group of children. There is no substitute for good organisation, and even 10 minutes each day spent making sure everything is ready and in place can mean the difference between children learning and children being bored and disruptive.

Another way is to give the teaching assistants some quality training on how to work with children effectively. However enthusiastic and confident they are, they are not teachers and will benefit from you passing on some strategies, e.g. be consistent in your expectations of learning and behaviour, establish regular routines for working, keep the sessions moving at a lively pace. Time will be well spent in making sure your school's teaching assistants, as well as being enthusiastic, are clear about their role and are approaching their tasks in a professional and competent way.

Parents

It always pays dividends to involve parents right at the start of any new initiative involving their children. You can achieve far more with their support than without it. Begin by inviting them into school to meet you, the class teacher and the teaching assistant so that you can explain exactly what it is you're planning to do, how you're going to do it and why it will benefit their child. You can also enlist their agreement to ensure that any homework their child is required to do by the programme is done. Not only this, but you can offer tips and strategies for them to make the homework a fun activity that they can do together.

To sum up

All the initiatives described above have a part to play in helping you raise standards of literacy, but don't forget that they have to be carefully managed in order for them to be truly effective. The key here is to foster professional and productive working relationships between your class teachers and the teaching assistants. The success or otherwise of the programmes depends almost entirely on how well they cooperate on planning and delivery. You might also want to set up separate display areas that show the work being done by the children in Early Literacy Support, Additional Literacy Support and Further Literacy Support. This will help to give it value and status and thereby act as a motivating factor for everyone involved.

PREPARING YOURSELF FOR OFSTED

The thought of an impending Ofsted inspection is enough to send a shiver down the spine of even the most efficient and well-organised literacy coordinator. It would be nice if we could look on it as an opportunity to show to a critical but fair group of fellow professionals just what we have achieved, but somehow that's not how it works. To quote one fantastic literacy coordinator of my acquaintance, who works in a brilliant school and should welcome inspection with open arms, 'Dreadful news, we've just heard we're to be Ofstedded – though I'm sure that shouldn't be a verb!'

So you're the literacy coordinator and, like my acquaintance, you're expecting a visit from the inspection team. (Even if you're not now, you will be at some point, so *do not* skip to the next section. You'll regret it if you do). Should you panic? The short answer is no. Remember, the inspection team can only make an assessment of your school based on what it sees – so make sure it sees plenty of evidence that the children are achieving to the limits, thanks to the unstinting efforts of you and your colleagues.

The literacy teaching in your school is proceeding smoothly and you have all your plans and policies in place, but even if it isn't and you don't, there's still time to do something about it. If, on the other hand, you're reasonably confident that the literacy teaching and learning in your school is going to stand up to scrutiny, it still makes sense to run a health check on all your systems and procedures before the inspectors arrive. A literacy coordinator who is on top of his/her job leaves nothing to chance.

Paperwork

First you need to run a close eye over all the policy and planning, monitoring and assessment documents which relate to the development of literacy teaching and learning in your school. Try to imagine you're not the literacy coordinator, but rather an intelligent visitor from another planet (yes, a bit like the Registered Inspector) who knows nothing about how literacy

teaching is organised in a primary school. Now sit down and read all the relevant documents. Do they make sense? Do they give a clear and coherent explanation of how literacy is taught across the school? Do they make explicit your expectations for the children's learning and show how these expectations will be achieved? Do they show how you're using your delegated budget to fund the acquisition of appropriate resources and training to meet the targets you've set? Are your plans and policies consistent with each other?

You may be able to answer yes to all of the above (if not, at least you've just identified where to start putting things right), but now you come to the big question: do these documents accurately describe what is actually happening on the ground? Because it's no good having perfect paperwork if the teaching and learning just aren't happening. As one Inspector famously remarked after wading through some hastily cobbled-together documents, 'Hmm ...these policies smell of burning midnight oil.'

OK, so what documents will the Ofsted team definitely want to see? Well, it's a really good idea to present them with your own file as literacy coordinator. This should include:

- your job description
- the school development plan as it relates to the development of literacy
- your literacy policy
- the results of your literacy audit
- a position statement of what's been achieved since you started your post or since the last inspection
- a statement on how your school is implementing the literacy hour
- your literacy development action plan (with timescales)
- planning, assessment and monitoring pro formas
- schemes of work
- samples of assessed work
- examples of literacy lesson plans (both your own and colleagues')
- evidence of observations of your lessons by headteacher or others
- evidence of your observations of other teachers' literacy lessons
- a comprehensive list of resources
- library timetables
- evidence of research, training, initiatives undertaken, innovative practice by you and other colleagues.

If you have previously been inspected, you should also include evidence to show how you have addressed the issues for literacy raised by that inspection. You'll also need to be able to explain how you're using the results of assessment and testing as a diagnostic tool to inform your planning. But it's not enough just to present the inspectors with a bulging file – you'll be expected to talk about everything in it and show how all your paperwork underpins and supports the progress being made by the children.

Talking of the children, the inspectors will want to see portfolios of their work, and it makes sense to go through those portfolios before you hand them over, weeding out those pieces of writing that haven't been carefully annotated against agreed levels. Less is more when all the pieces included are dated and serve to demonstrate that the child is making measurable progress.

Other things you'll need to be on top of

Meeting with the literacy governor

You will probably have a meeting with your literacy governor at least once every term, but it is a sensible move to catch up with them as soon as you know you're going to be receiving an Ofsted visit. You need to make sure they're briefed on:

- your role and exactly how you've been carrying it out
- the parts of the school improvement plan that you're overseeing
- how well the children are performing in literacy
- how you're measuring and assessing the progress of the children
- what you're doing to raise standards of literacy in the school
- your plans for the next stage of your school's literacy development.

Classrooms

Make sure that displays in the classrooms reflect the literacy learning that is taking place. Ensure that the children's written work, whether in the books or in folders, has been marked in a constructive fashion which encourages the children and gives them pointers on how to improve. Effective marking of children's work is a vital part of spurring them on, and Inspectors will expect to see evidence that this is being done. It also helps if all the children can:

- give the name of some favourite authors (not just JK Rowling!)
- talk about a book or books they have read and enjoyed
- show that they make use of the class and school library.

Literacy resources

An impending inspection can be the excuse you've been waiting for to clear out all those battered and out-of-date books which have been cluttering up the school for so long. It's far better to have a few top quality books and resources that are being used to good purpose than lots of dusty old relics which inspire no one. However, after you have culled your resources you may feel the book collection is now looking a bit thin. If so, you might want to consider nipping down to your high street bookshop to see if they've any surplus point-of-sale material that they've been using to promote new books for children. Moreover, you could phone a few children's book publishers and suppliers and ask if they can send you any posters, and don't forget your local library. The librarians there may be only too pleased to help out with advice, expertise and resources in return for getting greater access to your school.

Teachers' records

With the best will in the world, sometimes teachers fall behind with their planning and record-keeping. You'll need to remind them to check that they are up-to-date. This is never a popular request, so offer to help anyone who's got themselves into a bit of a muddle. They may grumble, but teachers will always make more of an effort for someone who's prepared to roll up their sleeves than they will for someone who just makes demands on them.

Remember, nobody enjoys the thought of being inspected, so it's part of your role to try and keep everyone's spirits up. Focus on what they've achieved in literacy with the children so far, and let them know you see this inspection as an opportunity to show how well you are all working together as a team to raise the children's standards of literacy further.

RESOURCING LITERACY

When it comes to choosing the resources you need for your school, you should ask yourself: are they high quality and will they help us inspire children to read and write? The way to find this out is to conduct an audit. Ask your colleagues to audit the books and resources in their own classrooms while you focus on the library. This will save you an enormous amount of time and, with an Ofsted looming, you're going to need all the time you can get. But you won't make much progress if you don't have a clear idea of what criteria to apply when deciding what to keep and what to throw out. Therefore, you may find the following checklists of use.

Audit checklist

Factual books

- Do atlases show the world as it is today?
- If a book has photographs/illustrations are they old-fashioned or outdated?
- Is the language used appropriate?
- Is the information still accurate?
- Does the book show signs of being well used? (It's popular so keep or replace it)
- Is the book unblemished but with yellowing edges on the page tops? (It isn't popular so discard it)
- Does the book support the topics you're teaching?
- If it's a craft book, are the instructions clear and simply worded and are the illustrations helpful?

Fiction books

Foundation

Do the picture books have:

- strong storylines and character development?
- attention-grabbing illustrations?

Do the fiction books have:

- clear text that is easy to read?
- simple, enjoyable plots?
- texts with good rhythm and effective word repetition?

- illustrations that bring the text to life and give clues to the meaning of new words?

Year 1

If a book is aimed at independent readers does it have a straightforward story using words that will be familiar from everyday use?

Year 2

- Do the fiction books feature stories of some complexity?
- Is the vocabulary relatively familiar while including some challenging words?

Key Stage 2

Do the books:

- Match the children's developing language skills, vocabulary and attention spans?
- Have developed characters, plot twists and descriptive language?

Some people find it hard to throw books away and teachers are no exception. A particular book may have been their childhood favourite and, if they love it they will communicate that love to the children which is a good thing – so it should stay. However, some teachers will happily carry on using certain books or resources long after their sell-by date just because they've always done so. If this is the case with some of your colleagues, then you need to point out gently that, just as a garden benefits from careful weeding, so does their classroom library.

However, you can avoid this situation by incorporating, as part of your whole school policy on literacy, a method that allows you to keep your books and other literacy resources current and relevant. It's in keeping with the gardening metaphor and is called CREW. This easily-remembered acronym stands for Continuous Review, Evaluation, and Weeding. By using this method you will be able to constantly add to, remove from, adjust and interpret your school's collection of resources to fit the needs of the learners and the curriculum. This has the added advantage of allowing you to spread your spending on replacing resources in a planned and orderly fashion rather than trying to buy everything in one fell swoop – and that has to be better than having a painful, time-consuming and expensive clear-out once every few years or when Ofsted comes to call.

Handy Hints

- Keep on top of your subject.
- There are many different literacy strategies – make sure you know what they are and ways to implement them.
- Remember the importance of communication.
- Thorough preparation for Ofsted is vital.
- Resource literacy in full. Start with an audit and use CREW (Continuous Review, Evaluation and Weeding) to ensure maintenance of high quality stock.

CHAPTER THREE

ACHIEVING TARGETS AND STRATEGY GOALS

All schools are, by their very nature, unique institutions with their own ways of doing things, but since the advent of the National Curriculum and the National Literacy Strategy *et al* things have become a lot more standardised. There are certain things that the DfES and the QCA expect to be happening in all schools if literacy teaching and learning are to flourish.

You may feel that you are confident you know what is going on in your school, but schools are dynamic places where nothing stays the same for very long. Even in the most stable of schools children come and go, members of staff leave or retire and new faces appear to take their places. This can mean that you're making assumptions about practice which no longer hold true, yet you'll still be held accountable if your school fails to meet its targets. So let's take a closer look at the whole process of thinking strategically about targets and how these targets can be achieved.

STRATEGIC THINKING

Thinking strategically doesn't mean realising something must be done, calling a meeting to flag up the situation and then launching into a flurry of action and activity in an effort to be seen to be doing something straight away. What it actually means is:

- understanding how your school really works in practice
- analysing a given situation
- identifying a problem or problems arising from that situation

- communicating effectively and persuasively with key members of staff
- generating a proposed solution
- anticipating the impact of applying the proposed solution.

Therefore your strategy for developing literacy in your school should be based on an objective analysis of the situation as it exists. However, don't forget that, as much as we all try to be objective, teaching is an emotional activity and people will inevitably bring their subjective views into play. This is where you'll need to inject a healthy dose of pragmatism into your strategic thinking, and bring all your powers of persuasion to bear, if you're going to arrive at a strategic plan that everyone is agreed on and will implement.

This plan will determine and embody your intentions for literacy in terms of objectives (long-, medium- and short-term), action programmes, resource allocation priorities and evaluation procedures. Now this is all very well, but to create the plan, you'll have to think strategically and make decisions accordingly. This can be done by following these five steps:

- Describe the problem facing you.
- Analyse what the problem means and what its implications are for your school.
- Identify your options – there's never just one.
- Make your recommendations.
- Identify unintended consequences. Every action will have the potential to cause reactions you don't want. Take time to anticipate what these may be. A strategic decision will usually be based on the course of action that provokes the fewest unintended outcomes.

To summarise, all strategic thinking and planning arises from applying a mix of careful observation, facts, verifiable data and the professional experience and expertise of yourself and your colleagues to a particular situation.

It sounds straightforward, but after you've all engaged in the process you may want to create a strategy chart like the one offered below (*Box 3.1*) as a way of making your strategic decisions explicit:

EVALUATION

Evaluation is a powerful tool for affecting change. It can guide improvement as well as demonstrating its impact. The evaluation process begins when you draw up your strategic plan and should be based on:

- clarity of thought regarding outcomes
- the ways in which children will learn and literacy be taught

Box 3.1 Strategic Development Plan for Literacy

School numerical targets:

• • • •

Key Areas:

Overall targets:

Agreed Action	Person/s responsible	Resources required	Cost	Start Date	Review Date	Completion Date	Monitoring/ Evaluation	Success criteria

- what evidence you'll need to inform your decision making
- asking key questions and finding the answers to those questions
- gathering quantitative and qualitative information from a variety of sources.

If it's done correctly, your evaluation should give you the wherewithal to make specific recommendations for future action. But there are pitfalls which you need to avoid when you design your evaluation tools. Busy teachers won't thank you for asking them to fill in long evaluation questionnaires, so think hard about what it is you really want to know the answers to, and then figure out the best way to find those answers. For example, you might go for a mix of structured observation, face-to-face interviews, short questionnaires, work samples and test results.

It should be noted that there are two types of evaluation: formative and summative. Formative evaluation is designed to catch problems early on while there's still time to do something about them. Summative evaluations assess the outcomes after an action has been taken and assess the long-term impact that action has had. It helps those charged with achieving the goal to fine-tune their actions and build on knowledge and data highlighted by the evaluation.

Summative evaluation has been described as rather like doing intelligence gathering after a battle is over. This is unfair and misses the point. To be successful, you not only need information at the time when you can use it to influence the outcome (which is what formative evaluation provides), but you also need to assess whether or not you actually achieved what you set out to do, how much it's cost you to do it and what you need to plan next. Only the summative evaluation process can do that.

However, we're getting ahead of ourselves. There's an awful lot to be done before you reach the stage of compiling a chart and evaluating the progress made towards achieving your goals. The first thing to do, once you've got a handle on thinking strategically, is to identify what is really going on in your school.

A LITERACY AUDIT

Targets or goals for literacy should neither be plucked out of thin air nor exist in a vacuum. We all accept that some are thrust upon us from above and some are inherited by literacy coordinators when they take up their post. Neither situation is ideal, but in an imperfect world we must find ways of coping with the demands made on us.

Now, as far as possible, all targets and strategy goals should be arrived at as a result of discussions – led by you – involving all members of staff. Naturally, these discussions need to be more than a loose exchange of anecdotal information or a rubber-stamping exercise. To be productive, they will have to be informed by the results of a literacy audit carried out by you, in your role as literacy coordinator, to assess the strengths and weaknesses of literacy teaching and learning in your school. This will help you and your colleagues to prioritise the key areas for development and allow you to think strategically about how to carry them out. Only then will you be able to set the agreed targets and goals you want to achieve in these areas. And make no mistake, target setting is vital, because by doing this you will give yourselves a yardstick by which you can measure the actual progress made by the children in their learning, and your school towards its goals.

Moreover, in a classroom setting, it enables both teachers and learners to be more aware of the intended outcomes of the literacy activities in which they're engaged. This in turn helps sharpen up the teaching process and gives the children a greater clarity of purpose. To put it simply, we all have a better chance of arriving at a destination if we know where it is we're supposed to be going.

Things to look for when you conduct an audit

So whether you're a literacy coordinator who's new to the job or one who's been in post for a while, it makes sense for you to do an audit of the literacy provision in your school. If nothing else, it will give you an accurate picture of the current state of play. However, an audit is only useful if it asks the right questions. The following may help:

Does your school have:

- a literacy development plan with clear targets and a time frame? If so are the targets and schedules being met?
- effective procedures and tools for planning and assessment of literacy?
- a literacy induction programme for NQTs (newly qualified teachers) and teaching assistants?

Are your staff:

- aware of the current school policy statement on literacy?
- using the National Literacy Strategy framework effectively?
- incorporating relevant objectives into their planning?
- using appropriate and effective teaching and learning strategies?
- using Developing Early Writing, Progression in Phonics, Additional Literacy Support, Further Literacy Support and Booster groups effectively and where appropriate?
- marking work constructively so that children are encouraged to improve their standards?
- collecting annotated samples of children's work?
- working together to agree levels?
- applying the principles of shared to guided to independent work during the literacy hour?

- teaching to clearly stated objectives?
- explicitly teaching key literacy skills?
- enjoying teaching literacy?

Does your school ensure:

- adequate time for reflection, review and evaluation to support assessment for learning?
- adequate time for teaching assistants to plan with teachers in order to increase the value of their support?
- information about children's literacy needs is shared with the SENCO and parents?
- staff receive regular and appropriate training on innovations and initiatives in teaching literacy?

Are the children:

- motivated to learn?
- making the progress expected?
- reading a wide range of books for pleasure?
- able to use the school library appropriately?

Are your school's literacy resources:

- of good quality?
- sufficient to deliver the curriculum?
- well organised?
- up-to-date?

Biting off more than you can chew

One result of asking all the questions above could be that you've discovered so many areas that need attention that you don't know where to begin to put things right. If this is the case, then it's a sensible idea to just pick one key area to focus on. The chances are you'll be far more likely to achieve some measurable success if you concentrate on managing one issue rather than trying to do too much all at once.

A preventative strategy

Once you've carried out the audit, you need to communicate your findings to the staff. This is where your ability to think strategically comes into play again because, of course, they may not all agree with what you've discovered and challenge some of your conclusions. Be prepared to listen to what they have to say. Your audit won't be infallible and you'll achieve more by entering into a constructive dialogue than by presenting your findings as a fait accompli.

However, this doesn't mean you're going to roll over at the first sign of opposition. Therefore, be ready and able to present the staff with evidence to back up what you say. But remember, no one appreciates having their perceived shortcomings exposed, and you certainly won't be able to start agreeing targets and goals in an atmosphere of calm and consensus if the meeting degenerates into a bitter argument. So it's wise to anticipate any problems (remember step five of our model for thinking strategically) and deal with them before going public with your results. For example, if one of your staff is not making time to plan properly with their teaching assistant, then you could arrange to speak privately to the teacher in question well before the scheduled staff meeting in an attempt to resolve the problem.

SMART TARGETS

There are fundamental principles that underpin the process of target setting, whether the targets are for individual children's writing, reorganising the school library or raising standards of literacy across the whole school. Their sole purpose should be to build on and improve the current situation. In your case it's to make sure that everything you do actively assists the children to extend and deepen their knowledge, skills and understanding of literacy. Therefore the targets need to be SMART. This acronym can be broken down as follows:

- Specific/small
- Measurable
- Achievable
- Realistic
- Time-framed

What this means in practice is that:

- If a target is too wide and involved to be completed in a reasonable period of time, then it is unlikely to ever be completed as other priorities supersede it or people lose interest.
- If a target or goal is too abstract then it will be impossible to measure.
- If a target is too complex to be easily understood, then it isn't likely to be achievable.
- If a target makes impossible demands on resources, then it is unrealistic.
- If a target is to be achieved then it needs a deadline, so everyone knows when it is to be completed and progress made will be reviewed at regular intervals.

As has been explained, the whole point of strategic planning is to understand the nature of an issue and then find an appropriate response. Well, you have used your audit to inform the discussion about the issue of raising the standards of literacy in your school; you've identified the challenges and now you've resolved to set appropriate targets as your response. Obviously, different purposes will require different targets and goals, but the SMART principle should be universal as it will help you achieve success.

Getting down to it

Right. You've thought strategically; you've completed the audit; you've communicated your findings and set your goals and targets. What do you need to do now to make things happen? Well, here is a list of actions that you can take:

If your overall target is to improve the children's reading skills:

1. Arrange an INSET on 'The Teaching of Reading.'
   Your aims for this might include:

- identifying successful strategies
- assessing how teaching assistants can be used effectively to promote the development of reading
- identifying appropriate resources to promote each type of reading, for example shared or guided
- considering record keeping and assessment
- reviewing how the library is used.

2. Buy resources for classes, e.g. guided reading books, books for class book corners.
3. Monitor reading records.
4. Use the reading records as a basis to set new reading targets.
5. Observe guided reading sessions.

6. Rewrite the school library policy in the light of the INSET discussion.
7. Assess to what extent the successful reading strategies identified are being used throughout the school.

If your overall target is to improve the children's writing skills:

1. Organise a series of staff meetings, each one highlighting a different aspect of writing, e.g. narrative or factual.
2. Use staff meeting time to monitor writing samples and agree targets for improving writing.
3. Assess the children's writing on a regular basis, e.g. every term.
4. Use these assessments as the basis for setting the next term's writing targets.
5. Keep the work in individual portfolios in order to build up a body of evidence that shows how the children are progressing.
6. Observe colleagues teaching shared and guided writing sessions.
7. Give feedback on these observations.
8. Collect evidence that your teachers are incorporating the strategies demonstrated in the staff meetings to improve the quality of their teaching.
9. Agree and implement a whole school policy on handwriting.
10. Buy resources to support the development of writing.

If your overall target is to improve the children's speaking and listening skills:

1. Arrange an INSET on how to use drama strategies and techniques, e.g. hot-seating or conscience alley, to promote speaking and listening skills.

Box 3.2 Literacy action plan for .....

School numerical targets:

Overall targets:

-
-
-

Agreed Action	Person/s responsible	Resources required	Cost	Start Date	Review Date	Completion Date	Monitoring/ Evaluation	Success criteria

2. Work alongside colleagues when they implement these techniques so that they have the confidence to develop them.
3. Organise a programme of visits to the school by writers, poets and storytellers.
4. Buy resources such as Oxford University Press' 'eQuest' or Sherston Software's 'The Crystal Rainforest' to support speaking and listening activities.

Finally, it's a good idea to draw up 'mini' literacy action plans (*Box 3.2*) for each generic area as well as having your overall literacy development strategy plan. You can display these prominently in the staff room (as well as keeping copies in your own literacy coordinator's folder) so that they serve as a permanent reminder to the staff of what has been agreed.

Handy Hints

- Strategic thinking is important – use a five-step model for strategic decision-making.

- A literacy audit will give you key information on which to base your literacy strategic development plan.

- Targets must be SMART.

- Evaluation processes can be both formative and summative. They will give you the information to decide whether your success criteria have been met and what needs to be done next.

CHAPTER FOUR

YOUR TEACHING ROOM

Like it or not, as the school's literacy coordinator you'll be expected to be an exemplar of good practice when it comes to teaching literacy. Now the place where you'll be spending the majority of your time is in your classroom, so it should serve as a showcase for what you're doing. But don't succumb to the temptation to try and be a beacon of light dazzling your colleagues with your brilliance. You'll only alienate them and put yourself under too much pressure. It's enough that you are a competent professional, and your classroom should reflect this fact.

Talking of your colleagues, they, no doubt, want you to be someone they can rely on to provide them with appropriate advice, guidance and support on literacy whenever they need it. Naturally, this is what you try to do, but you need to guard against spreading yourself too thin. It's inevitable that demands are made on you that require you to spend time out of your class – that's the nature of being a coordinator, you can't do it all from your room – but then you face the danger of neglecting the needs of your own children and falling behind with the work you're supposed to do with them.

Now in order to teach your children effectively, you have to plan your literacy lessons, deliver them and keep on top of all the record-keeping and assessment required. This can't be done quickly if it's to be done properly, so you must make sure that you allow yourself adequate preparation time to do it. In fact, you could make a very strong case for saying that the education of the children in your class is your number one priority. They shouldn't suffer in any way because you have taken on the role of the school's literacy coordinator. Having said that, there is nothing incompatible with being a committed class teacher and, at the same time, being a successful coordinator.

Let's explore this statement further. At first sight it seems as if you are being asked to do the equivalent of pouring a quart into a pint pot. Other members of staff will be looking to you to show them how it's possible to do everything that's required by the National Literacy Strategy as well as to prepare, plan, teach and keep records for all the subjects on the National Curriculum. They won't be impressed that your literacy teaching is excellent if it's at the expense of everything else. To add to the pressure, they'll also expect you to observe their literacy lessons so you can give them feedback on how they're coping. Yet, you don't want to short-change the children in your class.

Well, your classroom is, in a sense, your laboratory. It's here that you can try out new ideas and innovative practice and extend your experience and expertise. It's human nature to be suspicious of new ways of doing things. It threatens our comfort zone and it's not for nothing that the saying 'if it ain't broke, don't fix it' is such a popular one. However, if you can make an unfamiliar strategy work in your class so that children are learning more effectively than they were before, then the chances are it will have the same effect in somebody else's class. Therefore, you can recommend it to them, confident in the knowledge that it has been fully tested by you and your children.

Frankly, any innovation in teaching literacy is more likely to be taken up by your fellow teachers if they can see it in action and producing results – and your classroom is the ideal place for this to happen. This means that you are not always going out to others, but that they are coming to you. Your children benefit by having you spend more time teaching them and your colleagues benefit by seeing good practice being modelled in situ.

Of course, it's not always about persuading, cajoling and encouraging reluctant and overworked colleagues to take on yet another initiative. Sometimes your task is to respond to a colleague who is looking to be enthused or who just wants a fresh approach for teaching a particular aspect of literacy. Again, your teaching in your class will be the source of inspiration that you draw on to give them what they need.

Whichever way you slice it, your classroom, and the literacy teaching you do in it, need to be exemplary if you are to carry out your role in a way that satisfies everyone, including you.

WHAT SHOULD YOUR CLASSROOM LOOK LIKE?

Now we've reconciled the apparent dichotomy between being an effective literacy coordinator and an equally effective class teacher, we need to ask ourselves what your 'literacy laboratory' looks like. Ideally, your classroom should tell anyone who walks into it that you care about literacy. It should be a place that is organised to promote the kind of collaborative and independent learning envisioned by the National Literacy Strategy. Therefore the children's desks shouldn't be in rows, but arranged to allow for whole class teaching, small group work, and paired and individual activities, as well as for teacher–child reading and writing conferences.

The displays should contain challenging questions designed to involve children and make them think. These displays should be changed regularly and provide a showcase for the children's literacy learning. Although there is a place for posters and similar material, it is the children's work that should take pride of place.

A wide variety of books should be very much in evidence as it's important that you create a print-rich environment for your children. As we know, children have to spend plenty of time actually engaged in the act of reading if they're to become proficient readers, so you'll want to create as many opportunities as you can for the children to read in class. And what better way than to offer them a classroom where books and the written word are valued?

Not only this, but research has shown that, in general, girls tend to write more than boys. They are also more able to write independently and find it easier to initiate writing activities than boys. Therefore your classroom practice should take this into account by allowing both boys and girls the freedom to explore different texts in different ways, while, at the same time, giving them lots of very structured and focused opportunities to talk and write together about why and what they're reading. In this way you'll establish a reading culture that recognises, embraces and extends the range of all the children's reading interests.

Moreover, if your class has children for whom English is an additional language, then your classroom must reflect this by having dual language books and labels in the children's home language so that it is representative of the communities served by your school. This is essential, as children need to see the connections between who they are and what they're learning in school, so they can make sense of that learning and thereby internalise it. This is known as identity engagement and it's a vital factor in language development.

So let's summarise the type of print resources that any visitor to your classroom will see.

- a range of texts which supports learning across the curriculum
- a first class selection of novels, poetry books and anthologies by well-known children's authors from both the past and the present
- a variety of up-to-date popular texts to grab even reluctant readers, e.g. graphic novels, comics, sport and hobby magazines
- current reference materials, e.g. dictionaries (both simple and advanced), thesauri, atlases, encyclopaedias, globes, maps and holiday brochures

- books in the first languages of the children as well as dual-language books
- graphic texts like those the children meet in everyday life, e.g. menus, posters and signs
- wall charts, flow charts, family trees and graphs
- word banks
- instructions with appropriate visual cues, e.g. prompts on spelling, grammar, reading and proofreading strategies.

Classroom resources

But, of course, books and wall displays are not the only places where the children in your class should experience the written word. It's not enough to provide the children with a feast of print unless you show them how to interact with it. Literacy is a living, dynamic thing and children become literate, not by sitting passively while you transmit facts to them, but through engaging in activities which demand that they use specific literacy skills in new and ever more challenging ways. To do this, the children need a range of things such as CD ROMs, computers, science experiments, arts and crafts and design and technology projects, drama presentations, musical instruments and enquiry-based maths problems. These will give the children real reasons to read, write, think, listen and speak. For example, you can bring literacy alive for the children by using:

- props, costumes and atmospheric music as stimuli to dramatise scenes from stories and poems
- art and craft materials to paint, draw or even make models to express what they feel about a character or a story
- musical and percussion instruments to their own soundtracks to enhance a performance of a poem or dramatisation.

These days no classroom is complete without at least one computer with a word processing package. Some even have internet access and an e-mail facility. You can use your computers to support reading development by:

- motivating reluctant readers
- allowing children to experience texts in a variety of different forms
- providing opportunities for independent research.

Writing development can be supported by:

- allowing the children to plan, write and edit on screen
- reducing the drudgery of redrafting
- motivating reluctant writers and those children who struggle with presentational and handwriting skills
- giving access to a world-wide audience
- allowing writing to be published.

Speaking and listening skills can be enhanced by:

- giving children the chance to discuss issues and cooperate with each other when playing an educational computer game or researching a topic on CD-ROM or the internet.

You'll be using all these resources and approaches as a launch pad for the children to think critically about what they see, hear and experience, and any person entering your classroom should be able to see at a glance ample evidence that this is happening.

Organising your class library resources

- Always set out the books and other resources so that they look tempting and can be easily accessed by the children.
- Arrange books and materials by topic and literary category, and mark books with coloured stickers to indicate level of difficulty.

- Give each child a strip of card with their name on it. Then, when they go to select a book, they can put the strip in the book's place. Now you can keep track of who has which book and they know where to replace the book when they've finished with it.

- Sort independent reading books into 'browsing boxes' with labels that say, for example, 'Quick Reads – for readers in a hurry', 'Riveting Reads – for readers with time to spare', 'Rewarding Reads – for readers who like to get lost in a book' to make book selection easier for the children.

- Have the children design, write and put up signs explaining how the classroom library works and the rules you've all agreed for using it.

- Let the children take it in turns to be the class librarian.

Three eye-catching ideas to promote literacy skills in the classroom

The Trivia Bulletin Board

A Trivia Bulletin Board is a great idea for encouraging children to read and talk. All you have to do is have a small display area on which you post fascinating tit-bits of information, e.g.

The Biggest Crocodile in the World!

In Normanton, Australia there is a replica of the largest crocodile ever caught. It is 8.63 metres (28 ft 4 inches) long. It's absolutely mind-blowing to see a reptile that big. This animal could eat a horse and still be hungry!

Add new trivia every day and you'll soon find that the first thing everyone in the class does when they come in is to make a beeline for the board. You'll have them reading, talking and keen to find out more. Ask them to search newspapers, magazines and reference books to find fascinating facts and strange stories that can be added to the trivia board.

Outlaw words

We all know that children become very frustrated with words that don't follow the rules of reading, spelling or grammar. A simple way that helps them deal with this is to make a chart with bars made to look like those on a jail in the Wild West. Now you and the children can put those 'Outlaw words' into jail where they belong. The children can use the chart when they come across any of these words.

Use CUPS to proofread

Accurate proofreading is a difficult skill for children to master – yet it has to be done. The CUPS method gets them focussing on one element of proofreading at a time.

C = Capital letters

U = Understanding

P = Punctuation

S = Spelling

The children write the word CUPS at the top of their page. Then they check each aspect of the proofreading process in turn. For example, first they go through their piece making sure that all the capital letters are present and correct. When they are happy that they are, they cross out the C and repeat the process with U. They continue in this way until they have finished proofreading their writing.

LITERACY ACROSS THE CURRICULUM

Literacy pervades all aspects of the curriculum. Only by increasing their knowledge, skills and understanding about how language works will you be able to help children make sense of the new concepts they'll meet in other subject areas. By integrating literacy learning across the curriculum, you'll enable your children to apply their literacy skills and strategies in many different meaningful contexts. However, many teachers fail to make this connection effectively and your classroom gives you the opportunity to show how it can be done. For example, in design technology the children could design, make and label a simple machine, then discuss and write an explanation of how it works. In history, they could read about how children were treated in Victorian times and write a letter from the point of view of a chimney sweep. Judicious use of writing frames can also help children to bring their reading and writing skills to bear on a wide range of topics, e.g.

Our Mini Beast Safari

In the school garden we found:	In the pond we found:
Choose one mini beast and describe it.	Choose one mini beast and describe it.

Use the reference books in the class library to find out more fascinating facts about the mini beasts you discovered.

Facts about:	Facts about:

So, in essence, your teaching room is really an extension of you, as it allows you to give practical expression to how you believe children should be taught literacy and, if you follow the advice and suggestions given in this chapter, this will be evident to all who walk into it.

Handy Hints

- Do not let your role as literacy coordinator prevent you from teaching your own class properly.
- Organise your classroom to reflect excellent literacy practice.
- Use your own classroom to try out new ideas.
- Show how literacy skills inform every subject across the curriculum.

CHAPTER FIVE

WORKING WITH COLLEAGUES AND PARENTS OR CARERS

One of your key roles as literacy coordinator is to 'secure and sustain effective teaching' as well as to 'provide the challenge, information and development necessary to ... secure improvement in teaching.' (Teacher Training Agency, 1998). In short, this means working hand-in-glove with your colleagues to support them in attaining the goals your school has set for literacy. But it's not just about the teaching staff. As the American educator, Dorothy Rich (1990) says, 'In this complex world, it takes more than a good school to educate children. And it takes more than a good home. It takes these two major educational institutions working together.' So in this chapter we will examine what you have to do to not only identify, develop and promote good literacy practice in your school, but also how to involve parents so that they can play their part as well. Let's start with the teachers.

WHY YOU NEED TO WORK WITH YOUR COLLEAGUES

There's an old saying that says 'change or die'. Well, that may sound a bit drastic when applied to schools, but we all know how ideas can soon become stale and even the best teachers can get into a rut sometimes. A dynamic school is one where the staff are open to new ideas, constantly striving to improve their skills and knowledge and always looking to do things in a better, more effective way. This may sound exhausting, but it is where you come in. You can manage the process of change in a way that stimulates your colleagues and helps them to feel more competent and excited about their teaching. They will certainly look to you to give them the lead because, if you don't, then who will?

What to do

In Chapter 3 I argued that to be really effective, literacy coordinators should conduct a literacy audit, analyse the results in a strategic fashion and then act on their findings. You will have already carried out the audit and, after seeing the planning and assessment and the teaching and learning, you'll have a good idea of what is and isn't working. For example, there may be a year group in which one class is achieving far higher standards in literacy than the parallel class, even though both classes have the same ability mix. Alternatively, you may see book and writing displays of a very high standard in one classroom, while in another you notice that the displays do almost nothing to interest and inspire children. Every school will have many different strengths and weaknesses, and your school will be the same, so I don't propose to give a long list of examples of what your audit will have revealed. But I will say that, even if you haven't carried out a full-scale audit, there is nothing to stop you from going on a fact-finding expedition to check that:

- displays are sufficiently challenging
- the library is timetabled for use by each class and that this time allocation is being used to support learning
- the books and literacy resources used by each year group are appropriate
- each teacher is planning and teaching according to agreed procedures
- the children are keen to show you their work
- there is a genuine progression in the standard of work being done by the children across the school.

Practical ways to support your staff

Lesson observations

To do this successfully, you will need to draw up a schedule for classroom observations. Many teachers find the idea of being watched while they teach an unsettling one. However, your colleagues will be less defensive if they have some ownership of the observation process and its outcomes. So to be productive, these observations need to be focused and agreed with the teacher in advance. They should also have a built-in follow up feedback session at which you and the teacher can discuss what you've seen and how you're both going to act on those findings.

Remember, your task is not to sit in judgment on what you see, but rather to note down exactly what is happening. You can then help the teacher reflect on and draw appropriate conclusions from your observations. Telling them where they're falling short will have at best a limited and, at worst, a completely negative effect. Be as quick to notice and note examples of something going well as you are to note instances of things not going to plan. Your colleagues are far more likely to be receptive to change if they feel they're doing something right.

In short, you want them to look on the experience of being observed by you as a positive one. After all, you're not an examiner, but a fellow professional who's giving them the opportunity to get some objective and constructive information which will help them to improve their performance as a literacy teacher.

Your lesson observation form could look something like this:

Literacy lesson observation form

Date:

Class:

Teacher:

Observer:

This observation is focusing on the following aspects:

1

2

3

Aspect	Observation notes
Planning	
Lesson organisation	
Lesson structure	
Lesson content	
Tempo of lesson	
Questioning used (open or closed)	
Quality of children's speaking skills	
Quality of children's listening skills	
Quality of children's work	
Quality of interaction/discussion: between teacher & children	
Quality of interaction/discussion: between children	
Meeting the children's needs	
Task focus	
Task completion	
Lesson aims and outcomes	
Use of other adults	
Use of resources	
Displays	

At your follow-up meeting give the teacher a copy of your completed observation form. Agree any action plans that you and s/he need to make in the light of your observations and the discussion. It may be that you've just witnessed an excellent way of teaching a point of grammar which other teachers could use and you want to share it with them at the next staff meeting. On the other hand, it could be that you've seen that the teacher lacks the expertise and strategies to inspire the children to write creatively. It really doesn't matter because, whatever you've observed, be it a strength or something that needs improving, you both should have gleaned some useful information which you can use to inform what you and your colleague are going to do next.

Attending appropriate meetings

Over the course of a year there will inevitably be meetings which take literacy as their focus, held between year group teachers or teachers managing transition across the key stages. It makes sense for you to attend them to give guidance and information.

You can also use staff meetings as a vehicle to lead discussions on key aspects of literacy or to disseminate information. These are also great opportunities for you to forge a sense of united purpose. Find an example of good practice from each teacher (not just the ones who have a talent for teaching literacy) and have a show and tell session where everybody shares their expertise.

INSET

You can use INSET sessions to help teachers explore and experiment with new approaches to the teaching of literacy in a non-threatening way.

Dissemination

As literacy coordinator you will be constantly looking out for good practice, whether it be in your own school or others', on Teachers' Television, on courses you've attended, in the TES or other publications. Your colleagues will not have the time to do this, so you can collate the best of what you've seen and share it with them.

Modelling

Analyse the areas in which your colleagues need some inspiration and then organise a rota whereby they can visit your class to see you put theory into practice.

Giving advice

Your time is limited and it isn't feasible for you to model good practice to everyone who wants to see how something should be done. So be proactive in suggesting courses, books, resources and appropriate support to colleagues who are in need of help with a specific aspect of literacy.

Maintaining resources

Unless your chair of governors is an extremely generous Russian billionaire, you will be operating on a finite budget. But your colleagues still need resources if they're to promote a love of literature and all things to do with enabling the children to become literate. Therefore you need to make sure that they have what they need to succeed in this aim. Sometimes this means making hard decisions, but if you work collaboratively with your colleagues when identifying which resources are essential, as opposed to those which are merely desirable, you should be able to fulfil this requirement without breaking the bank or upsetting people.

Lead by example

It is a fact of life that schools these days are in a constant state of flux. However much we might point out that change is not synonymous with progress, we've already identified the necessity for schools to evolve in order to avoid complacency and staleness. Because literacy is so essential to the wellbeing of our society, it's inevitable that people will always be trying to find new approaches to it so that it is taught more effectively.

Having said this, new ideas and ways of doing things can be unsettling so you, as literacy coordinator, need to be a settling, reassuring influence on your colleagues. For example, don't just confront them with a list of things they're not doing and attempt to address them all at once. You'll achieve nothing except make yourself unpopular. Neither should you offer your colleagues a method of teaching so revolutionary that they can't recognise where it fits into what they're already doing. Even if you think they are still using teaching strategies that went out in the stone age, be very careful that, in your determination to bring them up-to-date, you don't throw the baby out with the bath water. Always find something of value in what they're doing and build on that.

It takes time to get people to accept and feel comfortable with change but, by making haste slowly, you will ensure the changes you make will have a real chance of taking hold.

Moreover, always have evidence to back up what you're saying. Your personal opinion that it would be good to do something differently will not be enough to convince your colleagues. You need more leverage than that. Obviously, your observations will have provided you with a good starting point with the staff as individuals, but if you can lead by example, either by showing the work you're doing in your own class or by taking other classes for demonstration lessons, then you will be practising what you preach. And that is always impressive.

Parents as partners

Research shows that children whose parents or carers play an active part in their education do far better at school than those children whose families don't. This is because the most important factor in promoting a child's educational achievement is living in a home where learning is valued. This has more impact than class, race, gender or even economic status, and the earlier parent involvement begins, the more potent are the effects. Everybody benefits when you can rely on the support of the parents and carers. Children are motivated and make more sustained progress as learning is reinforced at home, and they see that their parents or carers value the educational experiences you're providing. Your morale is boosted because you feel confident that your hard work is being appreciated and getting results. So, ask yourself:

- Are you doing enough to make parents or carers aware of how vital their role is?
- How far are you involving parents and carers in your aim of enabling each child to fulfil their potential in literacy?

These are fundamental questions, and you really do need to examine in detail what it is you're doing in your school. For example:

- What do you do currently to involve parents or carers in their children's literacy?
- Are these partnership activities working as well as you would like across the school?
- Are some partnership activities working better than others?

If so, why?

- How can you extend or improve literacy partnership activities?
- Are you involving difficult or hard-to-reach families?
- What can you do to improve communications with, and involvement of, hard-to-reach families?
- What opportunities are you providing for teachers and parents or carers to meet, discuss, share information and learn from each other?

Positive ways of working with parents

To paraphrase Jane Austen, 'It is a truth universally acknowledged that parents want the best for their children.' This being so, you can generally rely on them to be receptive to what you're trying to do. However, they can be very busy people with many and varied concerns, and may not have the time to come into school for meetings or to offer their support as volunteers. Others may not speak English or, having suffered a bad experience with their own schooling, may be unwilling to respond to your overtures. Some may even take the attitude that teaching the children is your job and nothing to do with them. This is all part of the challenge you face when working with parents and carers. None of these challenges are insurmountable and there are lots of ways in which you can involve parents and carers – if you keep in mind that different situations require different strategies.

Communication

The key issue is communication. You really can't do too much of it. The onus is on you to send the message that you actively seek the participation of parents and carers and that the school will give them a warm welcome when they come. Why not send out a regular literacy newsletter? It could feature:

- reasons why parents and carers are so important in helping children read and write
- practical and enjoyable things parents or carers can do with their children to support and develop reading and writing at home
- book reviews and recommendations
- news about forthcoming visits to the school by storytellers, authors, theatre groups
- reminders of meetings, literacy open days
- invitations to special literacy events you've arranged for parents or carers
- word games and puzzles aimed at adults.

Recruit parents from different ethnic backgrounds to help you translate it into their home languages, so that everyone is included. These same parents can also spread the message by word of mouth that you value the contribution that all parents make.

Encourage your teachers to write a regular letter to the parents or carers of the children in their classes telling them exactly what it is they'll be covering in literacy that half-term.

It's also works wonders if you can call parents to tell them when their children have made some real progress in literacy. It may be that they've read a book with real interest or produced a piece of writing of which they're really proud. It doesn't really matter what the catalyst is – the point is to share success. It's amazing how even the most apparently indifferent parent or carer can be enthused by hearing good news, so take this opportunity to begin to develop a more proactive and productive relationship with them.

Thank you notes are another way of acknowledging the contribution made by parents or carers in supporting their child.

They take a minute to write, but have an effect that lasts for a very long time.

Flexibility

Try wherever possible to arrange meetings with parents or carers at a time that is convenient for them. They're far more likely to attend if they see that you are making the effort to meet them halfway.

What can you do about parents or carers who don't get involved?

It sometimes seems as if you're doing all you can to involve parents but some just aren't responding, so you feel like giving up. Don't. Your first duty is to their children and if you stop trying, then what hope is there for them? Remember, there's always another strategy. So ask yourself why these particular parents or carers are ignoring you. Is it because:

- they are socially marginalized, e.g. asylum seekers or travellers?
- they feel, for whatever reason, unable to cope in a school situation?
- they are disaffected and resistant as they are already heavily targeted by social services and have had negative experiences with them?
- they feel their home culture is not recognised or respected by the school?

It could be that in order to reach these parents, and you really should make the effort as their children are often the ones who most need the support, you will have to go to them or at least meet them in a neutral venue such as a community hall. This is not an easy option and needs to be approached with care. First ask yourself why the parent or carer should trust you. You need to be sure they understand your expectations and hopes for the outcome of the meeting. In other words, they need to know that you see them as part of the solution and not part of the problem. So make it clear that this meeting isn't about recrimination, but about hearing their point of view, listening to what they want for their child and investigating ways in which you can work together to achieve this.

It helps if you can approach them through a significant other, i.e. either a friend or someone in their community who they do trust and who has influence with them. Obviously, if that significant other has had personal experience of your professionalism and care, then they'll be a powerful advocate on your behalf.

Having said all of this, visiting a hard-to-reach parent or carer can be a daunting task, so it's advisable to prepare for it by:

- Telling your head teacher where you're going, who you're meeting and when you expect to be back. Make sure they have your mobile phone number.
- Make sure the parent or carer is expecting you. If possible, phone to confirm you are on your way and when exactly you expect to arrive.
- Have a clear goal for your visit.
- Don't go alone if you are worried about your safety or ability to overcome cultural barriers.
- Try to take someone (another parent if possible) along to translate for you if necessary, but if you can't find one don't let the lack of an interpreter put you off. Making contact is the key thing, not understanding every word.
- Agree at the start a reasonable length of time for your visit. Don't outstay your welcome.
- Bring something along to break the ice, preferably a piece of written work that the child has done or a book they're enjoying.

- Be prepared to listen as much as you talk, and encourage the parent or carer to ask you questions.

- Don't require parents or carers to read or fill out anything in your presence, as their literacy skills might not be up to it and they'd lose face.

- Try to secure a commitment on the part of the parent or carer to do one thing to help their child, e.g. ask them to show them their reading book.

- If you can, arrange another meeting or, failing that, a system whereby you can keep in touch with each other.

If you follow all of the above procedures, then your visit should stand a good chance of being successful and you will have the satisfaction of knowing that you are doing your utmost to help every child in your care, not just those with supportive families, become literate.

Handy Hints

- All literacy practice must evolve or it will become stale.
- Staff need to be motivated to cope with change.
- There are many ways to support your colleagues.
- Children whose parents or carers play an active part in their education do far better at school than those children whose families don't.
- Include parents as your partners if you want the children to achieve the literacy standards you have set.
- Effective communication and flexibility are the keys to gaining parental involvement.
- Hard-to-reach parents or carers must be seen as part of the solution rather than as part of the problem.

CHAPTER SIX

LOOKING AFTER YOURSELF

You work hard because you are serious about what you do. We all know that developing children's literacy skills and encouraging a love of literature can be more than just a job – it can become a passion. A well-known book reviewer once said, 'They pay me to read books and I pretend to call it work but it isn't – I'd do it for nothing if they did but know it.' Well, nobody's suggesting for one moment that you shouldn't be paid for what you do, but the chances are that, like the book reviewer (who must remain anonymous for obvious reasons), you're also doing something that gives you enormous satisfaction. Yet that doesn't mean it isn't exhausting. Not if you're determined to give children the head start in life which being literate brings them.

So the probability is that you drive yourself very hard indeed. In fact, you'll almost certainly make demands on yourself that you wouldn't make on others. This is all very well, but to do your job effectively you have to strike a balance between working hard and making time for your life outside school. Some people can't do this and take their work home with them, metaphorically as well as literally. This just isn't a sensible course of action, because you are far more likely to find a solution to a problem or come up with a creative new strategy if your mind is fresh and your body rested.

Not for nothing did our ancestors come up with the saying, 'All work and no play makes Jack a dull boy.' Therefore if you want to be a better literacy coordinator you must take this on board, because nobody benefits if you're off sick suffering from stress and fatigue. This being the case, let's take a look at how stressed you are and what you can do about it.

A STRESS SWOT ANALYSIS

You probably already know that a SWOT analysis is used by organisations to identify strengths, weaknesses, opportunities and threats, but had you realised that you can use the same technique to see how well you're coping with the stress of being a literacy coordinator? All you have to do is take a large piece of paper and four pens, each with ink of a different colour (one for each heading). Then divide the paper into four columns and fill each one in as follows:

Strengths

First of all write down all your personal strengths, the reasons why you and others, like the head teacher, the governors and advisors felt you were the right person to take on the role of literacy coordinator. Next, list your support network. This might include your colleagues on the senior management team, other literacy coordinators or local education authority (LEA) advisors. Finally, make a note of all the resources you can access, such as your allocated budget, LEA courses or relevant publications and periodicals.

Now congratulate yourself on having so many strengths – perhaps things aren't so bad after all.

Weaknesses

Think about the things you have some difficulty with and jot them down. Perhaps you lack the confidence to model a good literacy lesson, or find it hard to cope with the mountains of paperwork generated by the job.

Now look at the resources you have. Are they adequate for your school's needs or are you struggling to replace them with a budget that barely keeps the children in pencils? What about your working environment? Are you making the most of it? Could you do more to make it print-rich or is it a hopeless case? Finally, do you have the whole-hearted support of your colleagues, the parents and the governors, or do you feel as if you're fighting a losing battle to win their trust and respect?

Look critically at what you've written and ask yourself whether you're describing the situation accurately or being unduly pessimistic.

Opportunities

Here you need to focus on the opportunities that are open to you by thinking hard about your strengths. Do these good qualities you've highlighted have the potential to help you manage stress? Are there people whose help you could call on but you haven't done so yet? Could you delegate certain tasks to others, thereby creating time for dealing with more important matters? Are you taking full advantage of any courses on offer? Are you actually playing to your strengths? If not, why not? Are your skills and strengths transferable to other areas? For example, if you're good at storytelling with the children, why not use that skill when presenting new information to adults? They're bound to find it more interesting than looking at a succession of overheads.

Threats

We're not just talking Ofsted inspections here. Consider what would happen if you continued to ignore your weaknesses. Imagine the consequences to your career, your colleagues, the children, but most of all to your health, if you didn't take stress management seriously. It doesn't bear thinking about does it? So take a long hard look at what you've written. Do your strengths and opportunities outweigh the weaknesses and threats, or is the balance tipping worryingly the other way? Whichever it is, there are strategies you can employ to improve your situation. What are they? Well, we've already established that you need to have a life outside the school, but that doesn't help you cope while you're actually doing the job, so let's take a look at how you can make sure you don't burn out while still being a truly effective literacy coordinator.

TIME MANAGEMENT

As we've already seen, you have a huge responsibility to deliver one of the most fundamental aspects of the curriculum, and there can be a temptation to feel overwhelmed by it. This in turn induces a feeling of panic, which if not addressed, can result in you rushing around like a headless chicken trying to do everything but achieving nothing. So the first thing to do is manage your time. You can do this by keeping an activity log for a week. Note down what you're doing, when you're doing it and how much time you spend on it. This includes the time spent:

- taking breaks (these are very necessary to recharge your energy levels – almost certainly you'll discover you're hardly taking any, which is why you end the day feeling bad tempered and worn out

- dealing with paperwork (decide what's essential and what isn't – both sorts take up your time)

- meeting colleagues, parents, children and others who make demands on your time

- reading material directly applicable to your post as literacy coordinator

- doing administrative tasks.

At the end of a week analyse your activity log. It should enable you to identify just how much of your time is spent productively. This in turn will help you decide which tasks you need to give more attention to, which ones you can delegate and which ones you can eliminate altogether. Don't forget that you work more effectively if your blood sugar levels are replenished regularly, so if you see that you haven't been, make sure you schedule in breaks at opportune times. Of course some of you are already saying 'I haven't got time for that!' Make time. No-one is suggesting you put your feet up and read the paper for an hour, but even a couple of quiet minutes on your own spent eating a piece of fruit and drinking a bottle of water can have a major effect on your ability to concentrate and be productive.

Make an action point list

If you've kept an activity log, you've seen how you're spending your time and you'll have a good idea of how to organise yourself so that you work smarter rather than harder. But even having your time management under control doesn't alter the fact that you have a very demanding role as literacy coordinator. The chances are you're a class teacher with only a limited amount of time allocated for you to spend directly on your whole school responsibilities. So you'll have a massive amount of different and potentially conflicting things to do. I'm sure you can feel your stress levels rising at the thought of coping with it all. Well, there is a simple tool that can come to your aid in this situation. It's called an action point list. If it sounds straightforward, that's because it is. But, like all the most powerful ideas, it's obvious when you think about it. To make an action point list take a sheet of A4 paper and write down all the tasks that are confronting you. For example, you may have to:

- organise a visiting speaker to lead your literacy INSET
- review the collection of reference books in the school library
- plan a meeting with the key stage 2 teachers on teaching grammar
- run a reading workshop for parents of the reception children
- observe literacy lessons
- model literacy lessons
- monitor all literacy planning and assessment documents
- talk to the teaching assistants about taking over responsibility for developing the children's Speaking and Listening skills while the teachers have PPA (planning, preparation and assessment) time
- brief the newly appointed literacy governor about target setting.

Some of these tasks are more complex than others, so break them down into their constituent parts. For instance, briefing the literacy governor on target setting might break down like this:

- phone literacy governor and arrange convenient date and time for meeting
- write short paper (1 side A4) explaining rationale for setting targets in literacy
- collect and collate results of previous target setting exercise
- prepare explanation of how target setting is organised throughout the school
- prepare for possible questions or issues the literacy governor may raise.

If some elements still seem too large, then break them down again until you've arrived at a list of all the things you have to do. Now assign each task a priority rating from A (top priority) to F (very low priority). It may be that, on first doing this, you'll find that you've given too many of the tasks an A rating. If this is indeed the case then revise the list and be really strict about what task gets designated as top priority. They are not all equally important and your action point list should reflect this hierarchy. When you're happy that you've given the tasks the correct priority rating, rewrite your list accordingly and tackle them in that order.

Of course, you may prefer to have a relatively short action point list which covers the tasks for that week, month or half-term. Some of the low priority jobs can carry over from one list to the next. It's up to you how you want to manage them. However, be aware that as time passes even low priority tasks will become more pressing and you will have to assign them a higher rating. On the face of it, making an action point list may sound like you're just giving yourself yet another job to complete on top of everything else, but this isn't the case. Properly done, these little lists will help you to be really productive and efficient.

THE LAST WORD

As Frank Smith said in 'The Book of Learning and Forgetting' (1998), 'The teachers who get "burned out" are not the ones who are constantly learning, which can be exhilarating, but those who feel they must stay in control and ahead of the students at all times.'

So try to be a constant learner not a control freak, and do keep in mind you can only do so much to improve the way you work. But the fact that you've read this book shows that you are keen to really make a difference to the quality of literacy teaching and learning in your school.

You won't always get everything right, but then your reach should always exceed your grasp. After all, if you don't attempt something difficult, how will you ever achieve anything worthwhile? And your goal of being a better literacy coordinator is a very worthwhile goal indeed.

Handy Hints

- Use a stress SWOT analysis.
- Manage your time smartly.
- Make and stick to prioritised action point lists.

BIBLIOGRAPHY

References

DfES (2003) *Speaking, listening, learning: Working with children in KS1 and KS2*. DfES0623-2003G. DfES Publications Centre, Annesley, Nottingham

QCA (2000) *Curriculum guidance for the foundation stage*, QCA Publications, Sudbury, Suffolk

QCA, DfEE, Book Trust (2001) *Writing Together Conference Report*. Book Trust, London

Rich D (1990) *Megaskills: How Families Can Help Children Succeed in School and Beyond*. Houghton Mifflin, Boston

Smith F (1998) *The Book of Learning and Forgetting*. Teachers College Press, New York

Teacher Training Agency (1998) *National Standards for Subject Leaders*, TTA. London

Further reading

Hepworth-Berger E (2004) *Parents as Partners in Education: Families and Schools Working Together*. 6th edn. Prentice Hall, London

Powling C (2005) *Waiting for a Jamie Oliver – beyond bog-standard literacy*, National Centre for Language and Literature, Reading

Powling C, Ashley B, Pullman P, Fine A, Gavin J (2003) *Meetings with the Minister,* National Centre for Language and Literature, Reading

Soler J, Wearmouth J, Reid G, eds (2002) *Contextualising Difficulties in Literacy Development: Exploring Politics, Culture, Ethnicity and Ethics.* Routledge Falmer, London

Whitehead MR (2004) *Language and Literacy in the Early Years,* Sage Publications Ltd, London

Wray D, Medwell J, Poulson L (2001) *Teaching Literacy Effectively in the Primary School,* Routledge Falmer, London

Useful websites

All accessed January 2006.

Department for Education and Skills – *www.dfes.gov.uk/*

The National Literacy Trust – *www.literacytrust.org.uk/*

Literacy Matters – *www.literacymatters.com/*

BBC Schools – *www.bbc.co.uk/schools/4_11/literacy.shtml*

Literacy Activities:

www.woodlandsjunior.kent.sch.uk/Games/educational/literacy.html

Primary Literacy coordinators – *http://www.sgfl.org.uk*